McGRAW-HILL'S
OUR NATION, OUR WORLD

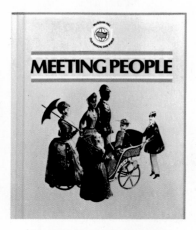

MEETING PEOPLE

School, Self, Families, Neighborhood, and Our Country

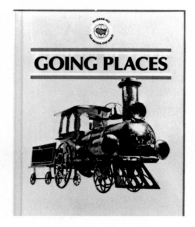

GOING PLACES

People in Groups, Filling Needs in Communities and on Farms

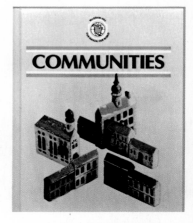

COMMUNITIES

Geography and History of Cities in the United States, Canada, and Mexico

EARTH'S REGIONS

Geography and Ways of Living on Five Continents, Studying the 50 States

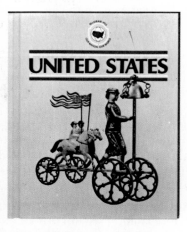

UNITED STATES

Chronological History of the United States, North America Today

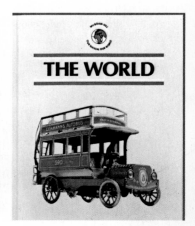

THE WORLD

World History, Ancient Civilizations, Important Nations Today

1

CONSULTANTS

GOING PLACES

BY Leonard Martelli, Alma Graham,
Lynn Cherryholmes

WEBSTER DIVISION, McGRAW-HILL BOOK COMPANY

New York   St. Louis   San Francisco   Auckland   Bogotá   Düsseldorf
Johannesburg   London   Madrid   Mexico   Montreal   New Delhi
Panama   Paris   São Paulo   Singapore   Sydney   Tokyo   Toronto

LIST OF MAPS AND CHARTS

ISBN 0-07-039942-5

CONTENTS

 1777  1795

1818

1861

6

1912

1959

MAPS AND GLOBES

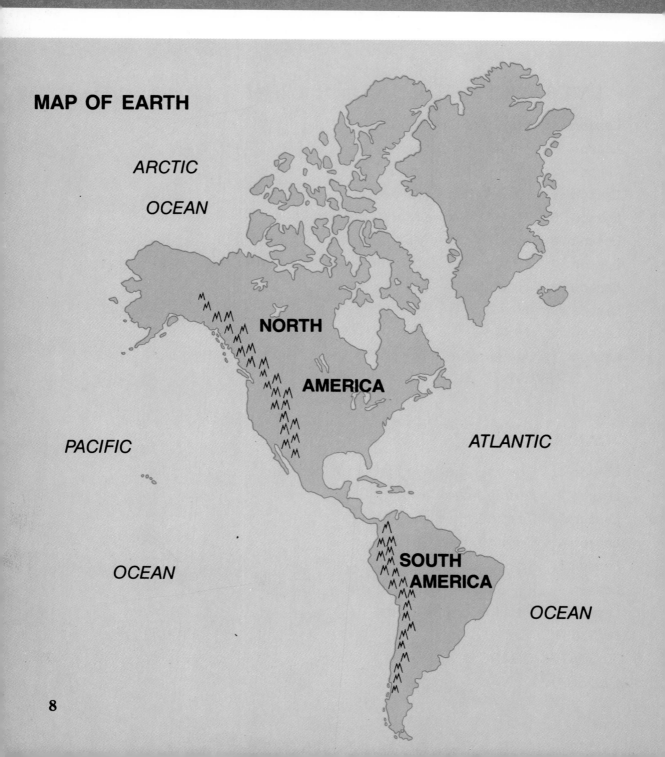

MAP OF EARTH

ARCTIC

OCEAN

NORTH

AMERICA

PACIFIC

ATLANTIC

OCEAN

SOUTH
AMERICA

OCEAN

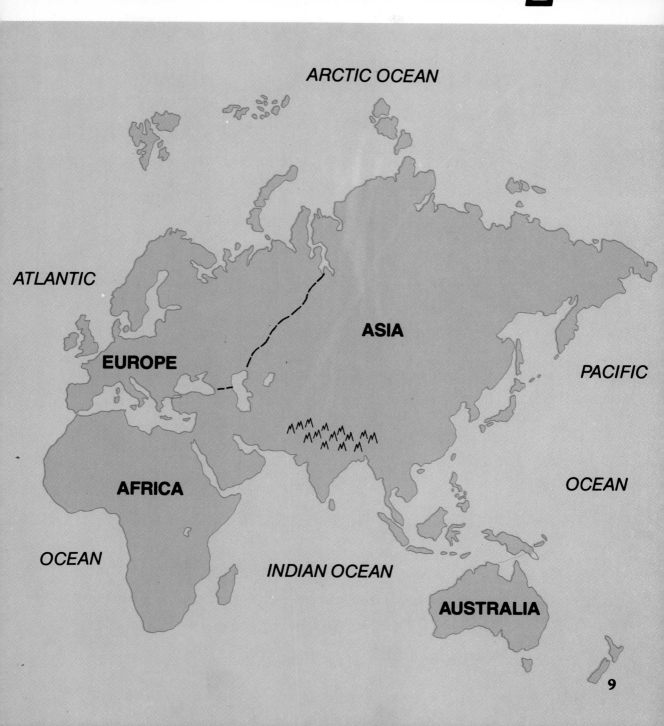

ARCTIC OCEAN

ATLANTIC

ASIA

EUROPE

PACIFIC

AFRICA

OCEAN

OCEAN

INDIAN OCEAN

AUSTRALIA

Lesson 1: A Classroom Map

These children are in school. This is their classroom. The teacher is Mr. Lopez. There are desks and books in the classroom. What else can you find?

This is another look at the classroom. It is
the view from above. Find the children's desks.
Find the teacher's desk. What else can you find?

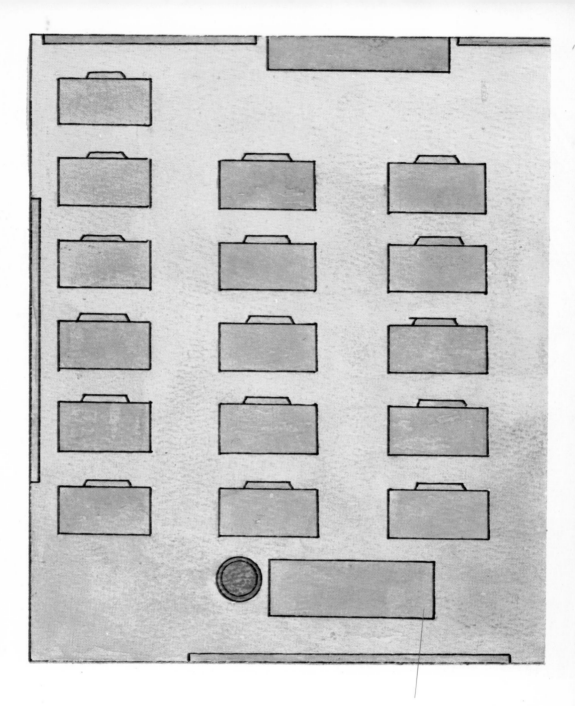

This is a map of the classroom. A map is a
drawing of a place. A map can show a
classroom. A map can show the whole Earth.

Find the children's desks on the map. Find the teacher's desk. What else can you find?

● What is a map?

Lesson 2: Find Your Way

On page 15 is a map of the whole school. You can use the map. It helps you find your way around. Find Mr. Lopez's classroom.

Pretend you are in Mr. Lopez's classroom. You want to go to the nurse's office.

You go out the door of the classroom. You turn left. You walk down the hall to the water fountain. You turn right at the water fountain. Straight ahead is a door. The door leads to the nurse's office.

Tell someone a way to go. Go from the principal's office to Mr. Lopez's classroom. Go from the lunchroom to the gym.

● How can you use a map?

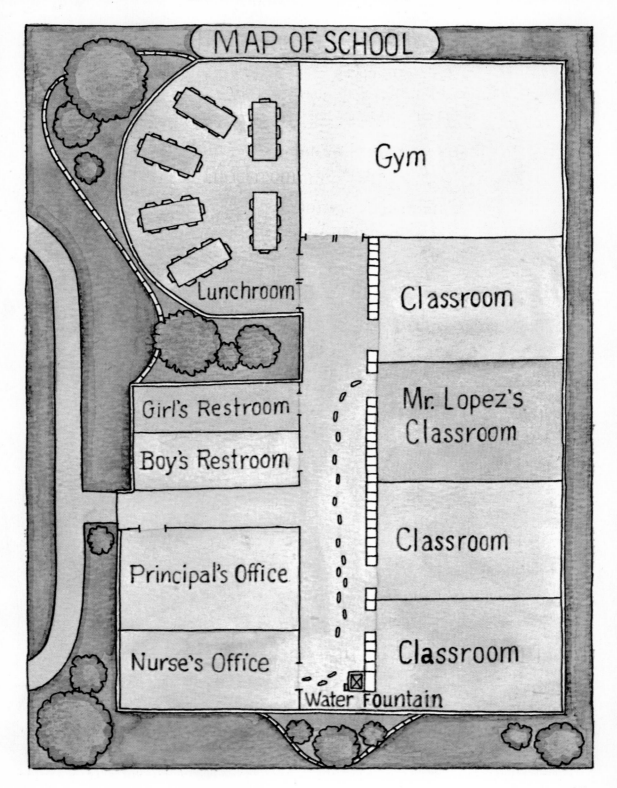

MAP OF SCHOOL

Gym

Lunchroom

Classroom

Girl's Restroom

Boy's Restroom

Mr. Lopez's Classroom

Principal's Office

Classroom

Nurse's Office

Classroom

Water Fountain

Lesson 3: Maps Have Keys

The school is on a block. The playground is on the same block. There are homes across the street. This is a map of the block.

Maps use symbols. Symbols are little drawings. A symbol stands for something else. Look at the map on the next page.

stands for the school.

stands for the playground.

stands for a home.

Map symbols are in a key. The key tells what the symbols stand for. Find the key on the map on page 17. What does each symbol stand for?

● What are symbols?
● What is in a map key?

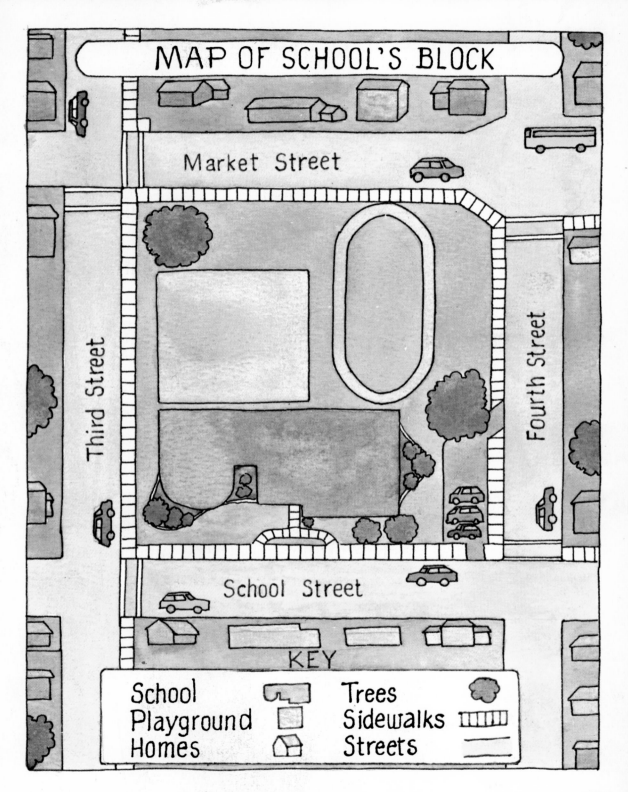

MAP OF SCHOOL'S BLOCK

Market Street

Third Street

Fourth Street

School Street

KEY

| School | Playground | Homes | Trees | Sidewalks | Streets |

17

Lesson 4: Directions on a Map

The school is in a neighborhood. This is a map of the neighborhood.

The map has a compass. A compass tells directions on a map. A direction is the way you point or move. North and south are directions. East and west are also directions.

You can use directions to find your way. Here is how to do it.

Pretend you are in front of the school. You want to go to the library. Go east on School Street. Cross Fourth Street. Keep going east on School Street. Turn left at Fifth Street. Go north on Fifth Street. Cross Market Street. Keep going north on Fifth Street. Turn right at Park Street. You have reached the library.

Directions help you find places, too. The bank is south of the school. The supermarket is west of the school. Now tell directions of other places.

● What does a compass do?
● Name a direction.

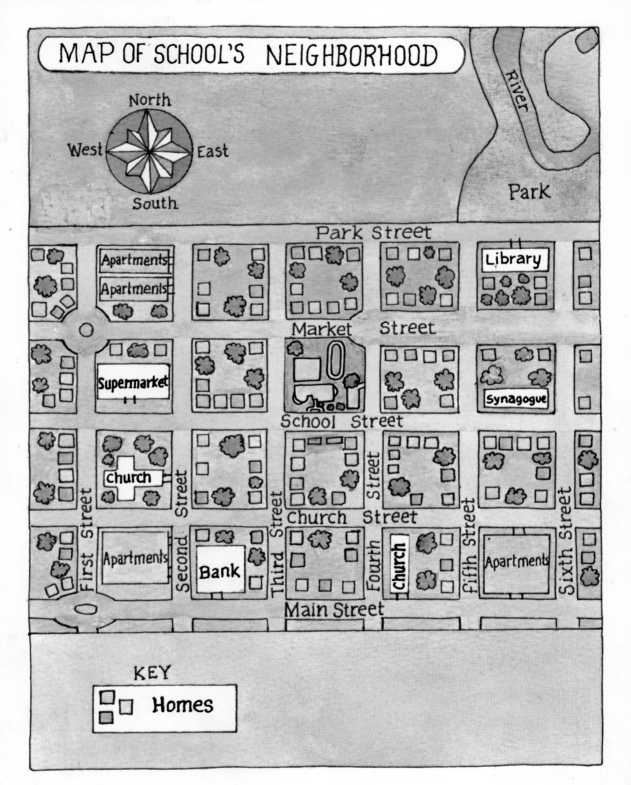

MAP OF SCHOOL'S NEIGHBORHOOD

KEY
Homes

Lesson 5: Maps Are Different Sizes

You have been studying maps. So far, each map has shown more land than the one before. The classroom is smaller than the school. The school is smaller than the block. The block is smaller than the neighborhood. So each map showed a bigger place. Each thing on the maps became smaller as the places got bigger.

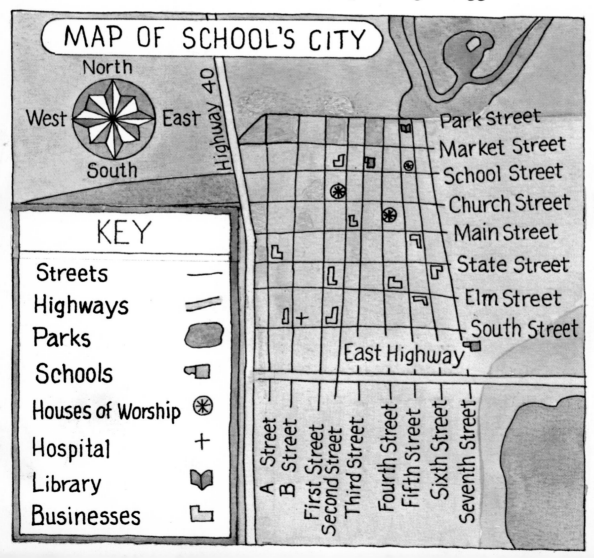

MAP OF SCHOOL'S CITY

North
West East
South

Highway 40

Park Street
Market Street
School Street
Church Street
Main Street
State Street
Elm Street
South Street

East Highway

A Street
B Street
First Street
Second Street
Third Street
Fourth Street
Fifth Street
Sixth Street
Seventh Street

KEY

Streets	—
Highways	=
Parks	⬭
Schools	⌐
Houses of Worship	✳
Hospital	+
Library	📖
Businesses	⌐

STATE OF CALIFORNIA

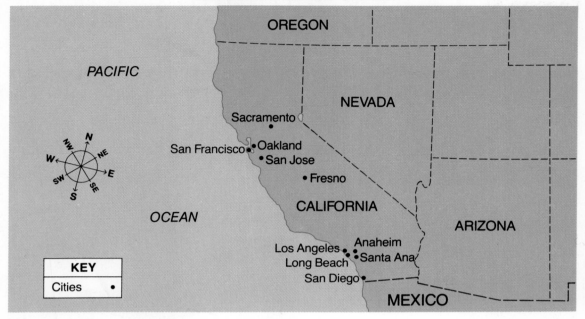

The school is in a city. On the left is a map of the school's city. Find the school's neighborhood. Can you find the school? What else does this map show? Find some of the same things on the other maps.

The school is in a state. A state is a part of our country.

Above is a map of the state of California. It shows some big cities. Can you find neighborhoods? Can you find schools? What does this map show? Can you find all the same things on the other maps?

● What is a state?
● What is California?

Lesson 6: Globes and Earth

Earth is our home. Here is a picture of Earth from space. Clouds are white in this picture. Land is mostly brown. Water is blue.

On the next page is a globe. A globe is a model of Earth. It shows land and water. Land is many different colors. Water is blue.

The globe shows other things. It shows the North Pole. The North Pole is the place farthest north on Earth. The North Pole is at the "top" of Earth.

The globe shows the South Pole. The South Pole is the place farthest south on Earth. The South Pole is at the "bottom" of Earth.

The globe also shows the equator. The equator is an imaginary line. It goes all around the globe. It marks the spots halfway between the two poles. The equator is at the "middle" of Earth.

● What is a globe?
● Where is the North Pole?

Lesson 7: Showing Land and Water

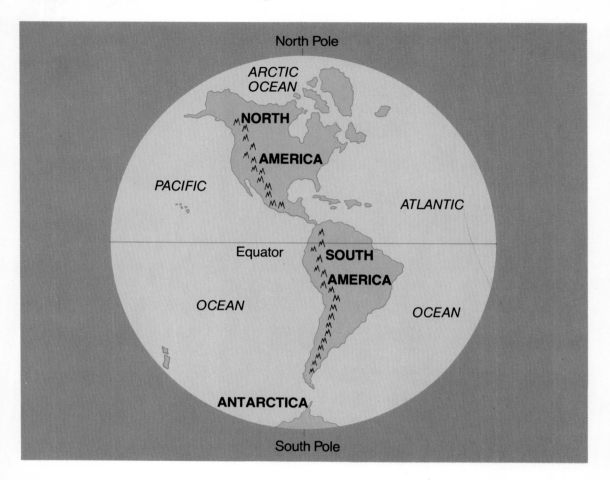

Maps and globes show the same things. Here is a picture of part of a globe. This is the western half of the globe. On the next page is another part of the globe. It is the eastern half of the globe. Look at the two drawings.

There are seven large areas of land on Earth. These are called continents. Each continent has a name.

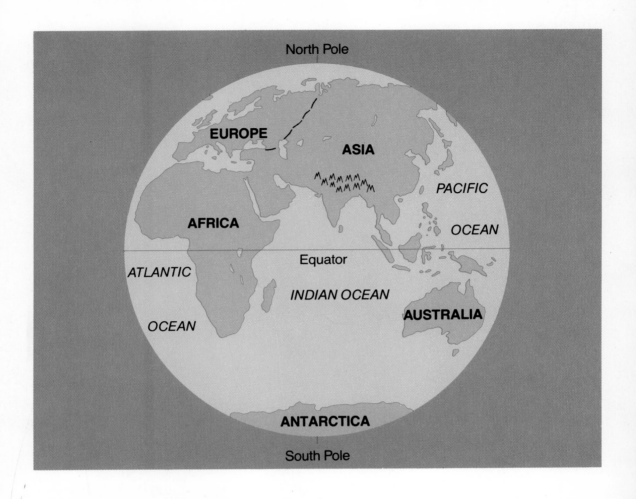

There are four large bodies of water on Earth. These are called oceans. Each ocean has a name.

Make a list of the continents. Make a list of the oceans.

● How many continents are there?
● How many oceans are there?

Lesson 8: Maps and Our Country

MAP OF EARTH

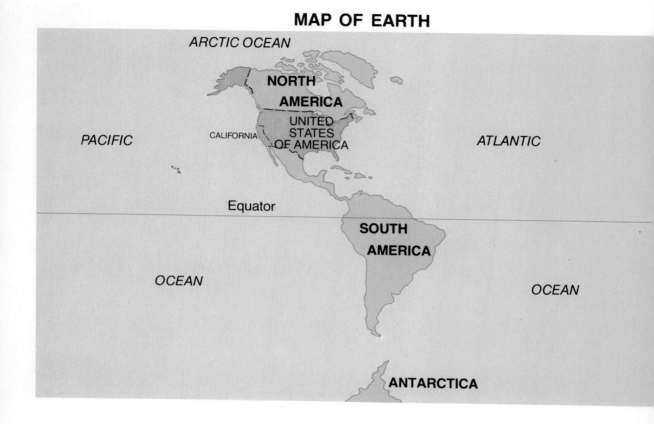

This is a map of the whole Earth. It shows all the continents. It shows all the oceans. It shows the equator.

Look at North America. North America is a continent. Part of North America is colored orange. This part is the United States. The United States is our country. Is our country north or south of the equator?

Four other countries are shown on the map.

MAP OF EARTH

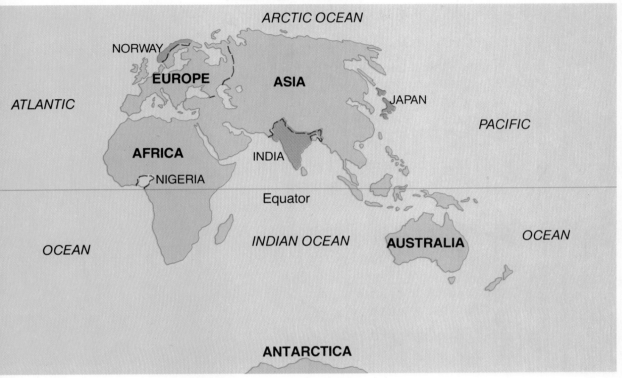

ARCTIC OCEAN

NORWAY

EUROPE

ATLANTIC

ASIA

JAPAN

PACIFIC

AFRICA

INDIA

NIGERIA

Equator

OCEAN

INDIAN OCEAN

AUSTRALIA

OCEAN

ANTARCTICA

They are Japan, Nigeria, Norway, and India.
Later we will visit these countries.

The state of California is also shown on the
map. California is part of the United States.
Look at the map of California on page 21. Is
California larger or smaller on that map?

● What is the United States?
● What is Japan?

UNIT REVIEW

WATCH YOUR WORDS

Find the missing word. Pick a word from the list.

key map globe
compass symbol

1. A___is a model of Earth.
2. A___is a drawing of Earth.
3. A___is a little drawing.
4. A___tells what symbols mean.
5. A___tells directions.

Find the missing word. Pick a word from the list.

ocean state city
country continent

1. A neighborhood is in a___.
2. A___is part of our country.
3. The United States is a___.
4. North America is a___.
5. An___is a large body of water.

CHECK YOUR FACTS

1. Can a map show the whole Earth?
2. What does a key tell?
3. What are east and west?
4. What place is farthest south?
5. Is North America a country?

USE WHAT YOU KNOW

Look at the secret treasure map.
Pretend you are at Silver City
School. Find the buried treasure.
What streets would you take?

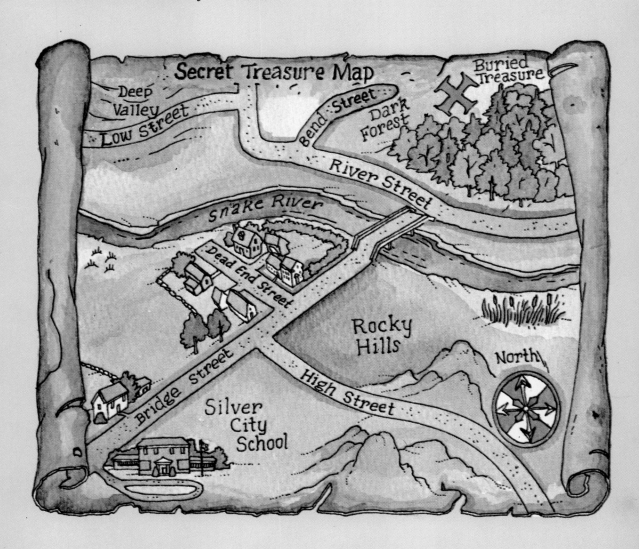

EARTH, PEOPLE'S HOME

Lesson 1: Many Kinds of
Land and Water

People live all over Earth. They live on land that is low. They live on land that is high. Some live near the oceans. Others live far from oceans.

Earth has many different kinds of land. In some places, the land is flat. Flat lands are called plains. Big parts of our country are plains. Find a picture of a plain below.

Some parts of Earth have very high lands. These lands are called mountains. Mountains are hard to cross. There are many mountains in our country. Between the mountains are low lands. These low lands are called valleys.

Some parts of Earth have hills. Hills are higher than the land around them. But hills are lower than mountains. Did you ever try to ride your bicycle up a hill?

Some parts of Earth touch oceans. These parts are called coasts. Some lands have water all around them. These lands are called islands.

Earth has many different bodies of water, too. You know about the oceans. These are very large bodies of water. The water in the oceans is salty. There are also smaller bodies of water called lakes. Lakes have land all around them. Rivers carry water from the land. They are long bodies of running water. The water in rivers is not salty. Most lakes do not have salty water, either.

● What are flat lands called?
● What parts of Earth touch oceans?

Lesson 2: Many Kinds of Weather

Look out the window. Is it sunny or rainy? Is it hot or cold? We often talk about how wet or warm it is. When we do so, we talk about the weather. Earth has many different kinds of weather.

In some lands, the weather is cool or cold all the time. These lands are near the North Pole or South Pole. So they are called polar lands. Below is a picture of a cold land.

In some lands, the weather is warm or hot all year. These are lands near the equator. They are called tropical lands.

Some lands are in between the poles and the equator. In these lands, the weather changes. It is not always cold. It is not always hot. These are called temperate lands.

What kinds of plants grow in these lands? It depends on the weather. In some hot lands, much rain falls. The land is covered with great forests. Forests are places with many trees. Hot, wet forests are called rain forests.

In some hot lands, almost no rain falls. The land is covered with bare rocks and sand. These lands are called deserts.

Trees need much water to grow. Grass needs less water. In some lands, there is not enough rain for trees. So there are no forests. But there is enough rain for grass. These lands are called grasslands. Grasslands cover large parts of Earth.

Our country is a temperate land. The weather changes a lot during the year. You will read about these changes in the next lesson.

● What weather do rain forests have?
● What weather do deserts have?

Lesson 3: How the Weather Changes

In many places, the weather changes during the year. So, we divide the year into parts. Each part has different weather. These parts are called seasons. There are four seasons. They are spring, summer, fall, and winter.

In spring, the weather becomes warm. New leaves begin to grow on trees. The grass turns green. New plants begin to grow from seeds. Some flowers bloom.

In summer, the weather is hot. The trees are full of green leaves. The grass is thick and green. Plants grow bigger. Flowers become seeds

or fruits. Some fruits and vegetables are ready to eat.

People enjoy the summer. They go to the beach. They have picnics. They stay in the shade to keep cool.

In fall, the weather becomes cooler. The leaves on some trees turn bright colors. Some leaves begin to fall off. The grass starts to turn brown. It is time to pick the rest of the fruits and vegetables. Soon winter will come.

In winter, the weather is cold. The leaves fall from most trees. The grass turns brown.

Cold winds blow from the north. Snow can fall.
People stay inside more. They wear warm
clothing when they go outside.

Some places in our country are different.
The weather does not change much. Some
places stay warm or hot all year. Other places
stay cool or cold.

● How many seasons are there?
● When is the weather cold?

Lesson 4: People Live on Many Parts of Earth

People live on almost all of Earth's land. They live in cold lands and hot lands. They live in low lands and high lands. People live in different ways in different places.

In hot, wet lands, people try to stay cool. They wear loose clothing or little clothing. They build homes with open walls. They may build their homes on tall poles. This keeps out water and animals. For food, they grow plants that need hot, wet weather.

In hot, dry lands, people also try to stay cool. They wear long, flowing clothes. These clothes keep the sun off, but let in air. The air

helps keep their bodies cool. People build homes with thick walls and small windows. These homes keep out the heat of the day. When there is water, people grow plants for food. Sometimes, they keep large numbers of animals.

In very cold lands, people wear thick clothing. They cover all parts of their bodies. They build strong homes to keep out the cold. They may hunt animals and catch fish for food.

In temperate lands, people have warm clothing for cool weather. They have light clothing for hot weather. They heat their homes in winter. They may cool their homes in summer. They can grow many kinds of food.

● How do people live in hot lands?
● How do people live in cold lands?

MAP OF EARTH

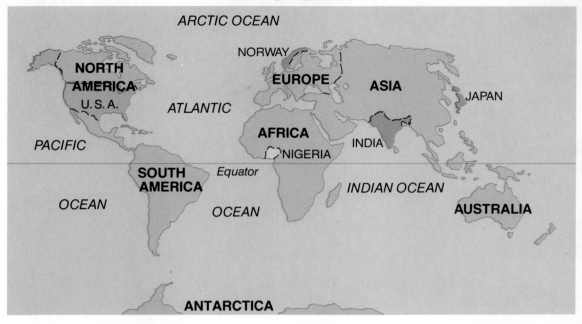

Lesson 5: Many Different Peoples

Earth has many different kinds of land. It has many different kinds of weather. People are different all over Earth, too.

This family lives in Japan. Japan is a country of islands. It is in the Pacific Ocean.

Japan is a very crowded land. Japanese people build very small homes. Sometimes, they use one room for several things. They might eat and sleep in the same room. They just change the furniture!

Sometimes, the Japanese dress in special ways. Sometimes, they dress just as you do. The Japanese do not use the same words you do. They do not use the same letters to write.

The family below lives in Nigeria. Nigeria is a country in Africa. It has hot, wet lands. It also has hot, dry lands. There are many different groups of Nigerians. All these groups do not use the same words. Sometimes, people from different places cannot understand each other. Nigerians also dress in colorful clothing. They build many kinds of homes. Some are very new. Some are for hot, dry lands. Some are for hot, wet lands.

The family on the left below lives in
Norway. Norway is a country in northern
Europe. It has many mountains and deep
valleys. People in Norway use words different
from yours. They build beautiful homes of
wood. Many people in Norway have light
hair. They have light skin and blue eyes.

The family on the right above lives in India.
India is a country in Asia. It has many, many
people. People in India build beautiful buildings.
They dress in colorful clothing. They speak in
many different ways.

● Name a country of islands.
● What is Nigeria?
● How are people in this lesson alike?

UNIT REVIEW

WATCH YOUR WORDS

Find the missing word. Pick a
word from the list.
Coasts Plains Valleys
Rivers Hills

1. ___are flat lands.
2. ___are low lands between
    mountains.
3. ___are high but lower than
    mountains.
4. ___touch oceans.
5. ___carry water from land.

Find the missing word. Pick a
word from the list.
season weather fall
Deserts Forests

1. Near the poles, the___is cold.
2. ___have many trees.
3. ___are hot and dry.
4. Spring is a___.
5. In___, leaves turn bright
    colors.

CHECK YOUR FACTS

1. Are lakes smaller than oceans?
2. Name the four seasons.
3. Do Japanese speak like
    Americans?
4. Where is Norway?
5. Does India have many or few
    people?

USE WHAT YOU KNOW

Match the names with the pictures.

Clear Lake
Pine Island
Snowy Mountain
Muddy River
Tower Hill

Lesson 1: Alone or in a Group

Sometimes, we like to be alone. We might watch TV. We might read a book. We might play with our toys.

We see other people alone, too. Some people work alone. Some people live alone.

But most of the time, we are with other people. We live with other people. We go to school with other people. We play with other people. Being with other people makes us members of a group.

We are members of many groups. Our family is a group. Our friends are a group. Our class is a group. Our church is a group. Our school is a group. We do many things with groups.

● Are we alone most of the time?
● Name some groups you belong to.

People form groups for many reasons. People can get things they need or want in groups. They may want to learn something. They may want to grow or build something. They may want to earn money. They may just want to have fun.

Children go to school to learn. They join sports teams to learn and have fun. They become Scouts for the same reasons.

Some groups last a long time. Families are one such group. Other groups last only a short time. A baseball team could be such a group.

People belong to some groups when they are born. They are part of a family. They are part of a country.

- Why do people form groups?
- What groups are people born into?

Lesson 3: Families Are Groups

Families are important groups. Families can have parents, children, and other relatives.

Most children grow up in families. Members of families help each other. They take care of each other. Small children need someone to take care of them.

Children get most of what they need in their

family. Families give children a home. Families give children food and clothing. When children get sick, their families care for them.

Mothers and fathers do many things in the home. They also have jobs. That way, they earn money to buy things the family needs.

- What kinds of people can families have?
- Name some things families give children.

Lesson 4: Groups Need Leaders and Followers

Almost all groups have leaders. Leaders help groups in many ways. Leaders help groups decide what to do. They make sure group members follow the rules. They give group members jobs to do.

In your class, your teacher is the leader. In your family, your parents are leaders.

Name all the groups you belong to. Tell who is the leader of each.

Groups need followers, too. Not everyone can be the leader. Followers help the group. They obey the rules. They do their jobs. They help out if they are needed.

Each person in a group has a role. A role is the part a person plays. A role is the job a person does. One person's role is to be a leader. Another person's role is to be a follower. There are many roles in groups.

● Who is the leader of your class?
● What does each group member have?

Lesson 5: How Leaders Are Chosen

Some leaders are chosen by group members. Each group member has a vote. A vote is a choice. The person with the most votes becomes the leader.

The President of our country is chosen by the people. Each grown-up has a vote. A team captain is chosen by team members. Each team member has a vote. Are any leaders chosen this way in your class?

Other leaders are not chosen by group members. Teachers are not chosen by their students. Bosses in companies are not chosen by workers. Teachers and bosses are chosen by other leaders. They are chosen because they can do a job.

Parents are not chosen by their children. Parents are leaders because they are older. They know what to do. They take care of the family.

● Are all leaders chosen by group members?
● How is the President of our country chosen?

Lesson 6: Groups Need Rules

All groups need rules. Rules tell group members what to do. They tell group members what not to do. Rules help people get along together.

Families have rules. Usually, children may not run and yell in the house. Often, everyone must have dinner together. Name other family rules.

Schools have rules, too. Children must be quiet in class. They must not push in the playground. Name some rules in your school.

There are rules in neighborhoods. Rules in neighborhoods are called laws. Everyone in the neighborhood must obey the laws. Stopping for a red light is a law. So is NO PARKING.

Name other laws in your neighborhood.

● Do all groups need rules?
● What are neighborhood rules called?

Lesson 7: Groups Change

Most groups change. In families, new members are born. Children grow up. Family members may die.

School groups change every year. New children start school. Some children move away. Every year, all the children get older. They have different teachers.

People change. Groups change. Places change.

● Do only a few groups change?
● How do school groups change?

WATCH YOUR WORDS

Find the missing word. Pick a word from the list.

rules votes groups
family leader

1. People form ___ to do something.
2. Parents and children make up a ___ group.
3. Groups have a ___ and followers.
4. Some group leaders are chosen by ___.
5. All groups need ___.

CHECK YOUR FACTS

1. Can you belong to many groups at once?
2. Do all groups last a long time?
3. Why do parents have jobs?
4. Is being a follower a role?
5. Name some leaders not chosen by groups.

THINK ABOUT IT

1. Why do people form groups?
2. What rules do you have at school? Name three.

USE WHAT YOU KNOW

Look at this neighborhood. How many rules can you find?

Lesson 1: Groups and Needs

People form groups for many reasons. The most important reason is to fill needs. Needs are those things that we must have to live.

Here is a way to think about needs. You need air to breathe. Without air, you could live no more than a few minutes. You need water to drink. When you run in the playground, you get thirsty. You can live only a few days without water. You eat food at least three times a day. You get very hungry if you do not eat. You could live only a few weeks without food.

But you need more than air, food, and
water. You need to be protected from the
weather. You need clothes to keep out the cold.
Clothes also keep the sun from burning you.

It is the end of the day. You need a place to
sleep. You cannot sleep outside in the winter.
You need a home. So clothing and a home are
two more needs.

Sometimes, you get sick. When you are sick, you need care. Your parents care for you. They call the doctor. They take you to the hospital if you must go. They feed you and watch over you. When you are well again, they are happy.

You do not have to worry about your needs. You know your parents will look after you. Your parents give you food, clothing, a home, and care. They take care of your needs.

● What are needs?
● Who fills most of your needs?

Lesson 2: Families and Needs

Long ago, our country was different from today. Most families lived on farms. Sometimes farm families helped each other. They helped each other build homes and barns. They helped when another family was in trouble.

But mostly, families filled their own needs. They grew most of the food they ate. They made their own clothes. They made soap for washing. They made candles for light. They chopped wood. They burned the wood to cook food. They burned it to heat their homes.

Sometimes, they had food to sell. Then they bought things they did not make. They might buy tools. They might buy shoes, salt, or medicine.

Today, it is different in our country. Most families now live in or near cities. Only 6 out

of every 100 live on farms. Many mothers and
fathers have jobs. They work away from home.
They may work in stores, offices, or factories.
They may work in schools or hospitals.

Parents are paid money for their work. They
use the money to help fill the family's needs.
They pay for a place to live. They buy food and
clothing. They pay doctors if a family member
is sick.

● Where did most families live long ago?
● Where do most families live today?

How Homes Are Made

You may live in a house. Or you may live in an apartment. Apartments and houses are both homes. But apartments are in big buildings. There are other apartments in the buildings. These buildings are called apartment houses.

How are houses and apartments built? First, someone must see a need. This person says, "New families are moving here. They will need homes. I will build homes. Then I will sell the homes. The new families will buy my homes." This person is called a builder.

Then, the builder needs plans. She goes to people who make plans. They draw plans for new homes. They answer many questions. Where will the living room be? How many bedrooms will the house have? Where will the kitchen be? How many bathrooms will there be?

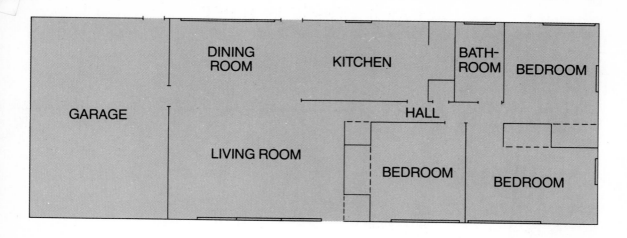

Soon the plans are ready. Then the builder hires workers. She will need many people. Building a home is a big job. She will put together a group. Members of the group have special jobs. Some work with wood. Some work with wires. Some work with pipes. Some work with bricks. Each person has a special job.

The builder must also get all the things the workers need. She must buy wood. She must buy pipes and wires. She must buy bricks and cement. She must buy windows and doors. Each of these things comes from a factory. At the factory, groups of people work. They make the things needed in homes.

Look at the drawings on page 77. They show how a house is built.

● What is the first step in building homes?
● Where are things needed in homes made?

HOW A HOUSE IS BUILT

1. Masons put a foundation in the ground. The house sits on the foundation.

2. Carpenters put up the frame of the house.

3. Roofers put on a roof to keep out the rain.

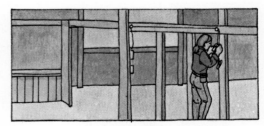

4. Electricians put wires in the walls for lights.

5. Plumbers put pipes in the walls. The pipes will carry water to bathrooms and kitchen.

6. Carpenters then finish the walls. They also put in the windows and doors.

7. Painters paint the house inside and outside.

8. Then the new home is ready. People can move in.

Lesson 4: How We Get Our Home

Finding a home is important. Families must answer many questions. Should they buy a house or an apartment? Should they rent a house or an apartment? How many rooms do they need? Where do they want to live? How much money can they spend?

Some families buy homes. They may buy a big house. Or, they may buy a small house. Then, they own the house. It belongs to them alone. Many families own homes.

But homes cost a lot of money. Some
families do not have enough money. Or, they
may not want to buy a house. Then, they rent a
house or apartment. They pay money to the
owner. The money is called rent. The owner
then lets the family live in the house. The
owner is the landlord. The people who pay rent
are renters. They are also called tenants.

● What is a landlord?
● What is a tenant?

Lesson 5: How Clothes Are Made

Clothes can be made at home. But many people buy clothes in stores. Suppose you need a coat. You go to the store with your parents. Your parents buy a coat for you. Buying a coat is easy. But many people helped make the coat. Many people helped put the coat in the store.

Here is a story. It tells how people make a coat.

Wool comes from sheep. Sheep are animals with very thick hair. Some of this hair is wool. Sheep are raised on ranches.

Once a year, all the sheep are gathered together. Then, people cut the wool off the sheep. This does not hurt the sheep.

The wool is packed up. It is sent to a factory. It may be sent by truck or train. At the factory, the wool is washed. Then it is combed. This is done just like you comb your hair. Now the wool is ready to be used.

Big machines, called spinning frames, spin the wool into thread. Some of the thread is used for sewing. But most of the thread is taken to other machines. These machines are called looms. They make thread into cloth. The loom

does this by weaving the threads together. Look at the pictures on page 81. Find the picture that shows threads on a machine.

The woven cloth is given color. This is called dyeing. Cloth can be dyed any color. The cloth is then sent to another factory. Now the cloth will be made into a coat.

First, someone must make a drawing of a coat. This drawing shows what the coat will look like. Another person makes a pattern. A pattern shows all the parts of the coat. The pattern is made in many different sizes. Some coats will be big. Some will be small.

The pattern is put on top of the woven cloth. Then the cloth is cut. After all the parts are cut, people sew them together. They do this using sewing machines. The result is a coat.

Many coats are packed into big boxes at the factory. Then they are sent to the store. There are big coats and small coats. They are put on racks. You find your size and buy a coat.

You see, buying a coat is easy. Making a coat is a big job. Many groups of people had to work together.

● Where does wool come from?

● What machines make thread into cloth?

Lesson 6: How We Get Water

At home, you can get water. You turn a knob. Water comes out of a pipe. Did you ever wonder about this water? Where does it come from? How does it get to your home?

Water falls to the ground as rain or snow. Some goes into the ground. Some goes into rivers and lakes. Sometimes, water in rivers and lakes is clean. Sometimes, it gets dirty.

Some water is sent to a water-treatment plant. A water-treatment plant makes all the water clean. It kills all the germs. Then the water is sent into big pipes. Some pipes are under streets. Smaller pipes are connected to the big pipes. These small pipes bring water into your home. Your home has pipes inside

the walls. These are the pipes that bring water to you.

What happens when water leaves your home? It goes into pipes called waste pipes. They connect to a big pipe called a sewer. The sewer takes the water to another treatment plant. There, the water is made clean again. Then it is put into a river, a lake, or an ocean.

Sometimes, water is not clean. Sometimes, water has wastes in it. This is called pollution. Pollution can come from many places. Some factories cause pollution. Cities can cause pollution, too. Sometimes factories or cities dump wastes into the water.

Some people want to stop pollution. They want to stop anyone from dumping wastes into the water.

● Is water in rivers always clean?
● What are wastes in water called?

Lesson 7: How We Protect Our Air

We like to think that air is free. After all, no one makes you pay for it. And you can have all you want. No one says you are using too much.

But air is not really free. We need clean air to live. Many things can make air dirty. You have read about wastes in the water. You know that is called pollution. Dirt in the air is also called pollution.

You know that some factories put wastes into the water. Some also put wastes into the air. Cars, trucks, and buses burn gasoline to run. When they do this, they make wastes. These wastes are also put into the air. In winter, houses and other buildings are heated. Oil, gas, and coal are burned for heat. This burning makes wastes. These wastes are also put into the air. Burning anything causes pollution of the air.

Some people are working hard to keep the air clean. They have formed groups to stop pollution of the air. There are also many laws against air pollution.

It costs money to make wastes clean. Factories must spend money to clean up wastes. So they have to charge more for things they

make. Car makers must build cars that make fewer wastes. This costs money. So cars also cost more. Building owners must spend money to clean up wastes. So they have to charge more rent. When people buy things and pay rent, they are doing something more. They are also spending money to keep the air clean.

But keeping the air clean saves money, too. Dirty air makes other things dirty. People have to wash things more often. That costs money. Sometimes, dirty air also makes people sick. They have to spend money for doctors. They have to buy medicines. Sometimes, they get too sick to work and earn money. So they lose money that way, too. Keeping the air clean costs money. But it saves money, too.

● What is dirt in the air called?
● Does cleaning up wastes cost money?

WATCH YOUR WORDS

Find the missing word. Pick a word from the list.

Builders rent Landlords
factories apartments

1. People live in houses or___.
2. ___make homes that people buy.
3. Things for homes are made in ___.
4. ___own houses or apartments.
5. Tenants pay___to the owner.

Find the missing word. Pick a word from the list.

cloth dyed Wool
pattern thread

1. ___comes from sheep.
2. Spinning frames make___.
3. Looms make___.
4. Cloth is___any color.
5. Clothes are cut from a___.

CHECK YOUR FACTS

1. Name some needs you have.
2. Do most families live on farms today?
3. Does cutting wool off sheep hurt the sheep?
4. What is water pollution?
5. What is air pollution?

USE WHAT YOU KNOW

Look at this picture. It shows some things you need. How many can you find?

Lesson 1: How We Get Food

You eat when you are hungry. You usually have three meals a day. You have meals at home. You have meals at school. You know that your parents buy food at the supermarket.

At the supermarket, you can buy fruit and vegetables. You can buy meat, milk, and cheese. You can buy baked foods. These include bread, cookies, and cake. You can buy canned foods and frozen foods.

Where does all this food come from? It
comes from many different places. But most
food comes from farms. Farms are pieces of
land where food is grown. There are farms all
over the world. People who own and run farms
are called farmers. Farmers grow many different
kinds of food.

We are going to visit several kinds of farms.
Some are in our country. Some are not. We will
see where food comes from.

● Where does most food come from?

Lesson 2: What a Farm Is Like

Some farms grow mostly one kind of food. These are large farms. They are called specialty farms. Other farms grow several kinds of food. These are called mixed farms. We are going to visit a mixed farm.

This farm is located in the state of Iowa. Iowa is a part of our country. The farmers grow corn and hay on the farm. They raise cattle, hogs, and chickens. They also grow some fruits and vegetables.

There are several buildings on the farm.
There is a house for the family. There is a big
barn for the cattle. Hay, or dried grass, is also
kept in the barn. There is a shed for tools and
machines. There is a pen for the hogs. There is
a small building for the chickens. There is a big
round building. It is used to keep corn. It is
called a silo.

The farm has several fields. Corn grows in
some fields. The corn and hay are fed to the
animals. The cattle and hogs are raised for meat.
They are sold in the market. Chickens lay eggs.
The eggs are sold. Some chickens are sold, too.
The farmers have a garden near the house. They
grow fruits and vegetables there. They grow
pumpkins, squash, watermelons, and tomatoes.

In the spring, the farmers plant the crops.
The baby cattle and pigs are born in the spring,
too. Over the summer, the crops grow. They are
harvested, or gathered, in the fall.

● What farm building is for cattle?
● What is done with the corn and hay?

Lesson 3: Farms of Long Ago

Long ago, farms in our country were different from today. Today, much farm work is done with machines. Machines help plow the land. They help plant and harvest crops.

Farmhouses today are as modern as homes anywhere. They have electric lights. They may have central heating and air conditioning. They have freezers, refrigerators, and all the other things. But pioneer farms were very different.

Pioneers are the first new people to settle in

a place. Long ago, pioneers moved to new parts
of our country. They were often the first
farmers in an area. Here is how many pioneer
families lived.

The pioneer family's home was made of
logs. It was not large. Family members cut the
logs. They made walls. They cut boards for
doors and roofs. They made shutters to cover
windows. Between the logs in the wall, they
stuffed mud. This kept the wind out in winter.
Sometimes, the floor was made of packed dirt.
Sometimes, the family cut boards for a floor.

The house had a big fireplace. The fireplace was used for heating and cooking. Big iron pots hung in the fireplace. Inside the pots, food cooked. Bread was also baked in the fireplace.

Pioneer families had to do everything for themselves. They made soap and candles. They made their own clothes. They grew their own food. They kept a few chickens and hogs. They hunted in the forests for meat and furs.

Most families owned a strong animal. It might have been a horse, mule, or ox. The animal pulled the plow. This broke up the soil. Then the crops could be planted. The family planted the crops by hand. They used hoes to

get rid of weeds. They harvested the crops
by hand.

Families hoped to grow more food than they
needed. Then they could sell some. With the
money, they would make life better. They might
build a better home. They might get a metal
stove for heat. They could buy more animals.
They could get better furniture.

Many pioneer families succeeded. Many
farms in our country today were started by
pioneers.

● What are pioneers?
● Did the pioneers farm with machines?

How Wheat Is Grown

Plants that are grown on farms are called crops. Wheat is a very important crop. Farmers grow wheat in many parts of Earth. Wheat is planted on more land than any other crop.

Wheat is like grass. It grows up to 5 feet tall. The top part of the plant is called the head. It contains the grain. The grain is the seed of the wheat. It is the part of the wheat plant we eat.

Spring wheat is planted in the spring. First, the farmers plow the land. The plow is a tool. It turns the soil. But it leaves the soil in big lumps. Next, the farmers use a disk harrow.

This is a tool that breaks up the lumps. Then,
the farmers use a tool called a drill. It plants
the seeds. The farmers pull each of these tools
with a tractor.

During the summer, the wheat plants grow.
The farmers watch for weeds. They keep weeds
from growing in place of the wheat. They watch
for bugs. They keep bugs from eating the wheat.

In the fall, the wheat turns yellow. It is then ready to be harvested. The farmers use a big machine called a combine. It cuts the heads off the wheat. It separates the grain. Then it pours the grain into a truck.

The truck takes the wheat to a grain elevator. There it is stored until it is used.

● What crop is planted on the most land?
● What part of the wheat plant do we eat?

How Wheat Is
Made into Bread

Wheat grain is made into many different
foods. Bread, cake, donuts, spaghetti, and cereal
are some of these. Much is done to grain to
make it into food. Here is how a loaf of bread
is made.

The grain is taken to a mill. At the mill, the
wheat is ground up. The ground-up grain is
called flour. You can buy flour in the store.

Bakeries make bread. They buy flour from the mill. They buy eggs and other things they need. They mix the flour and other things in a machine. This makes dough. Dough is bread that is not baked.

The dough is put into big baskets. It rises, or gets bigger. Then it is put into another machine. This machine cuts it into loaves. The loaves are put into pans. They are left to rise some more.

When the dough has risen enough, it is baked. This is done in a big oven. The oven bakes the bread.

When the bread is baked, it is left to cool. Then it is cut into slices and wrapped with paper.

Later, trucks carry the bread to supermarkets. There, your parents buy it. With the bread, you can make a peanut-butter sandwich.

So now you know the story of wheat. You know how bread is made.

● What is ground-up grain called?
● Where is bread made?

Lesson 6: How We Get Milk

A dairy farm is a special kind of farm. Dairy farms keep dairy cattle. These are cows that give milk. From milk we make cream, butter, cheese, and other things.

There are several buildings on a dairy farm. One is a milking barn. It is a big building with a stall for each cow. A cow knows its stall and goes to it. In the milking barn, there is a milking machine. It takes milk from the cow.

The milking barn is kept very clean. It is washed every day. The cows are also washed before they are milked. The milk from the cows does not touch the air. It goes through glass pipes to a big tank. In this tank, the milk is cooled. The tank is in a building called a milk house. After the milking is over, the pipes are washed.

The cows are milked very early in the morning. In warm weather, they may spend the day in the fields. There, they eat grass all day. In cold weather, they are kept in another barn. It is called a loafing barn. There, they eat hay all day. In the evening, the cows are milked again.

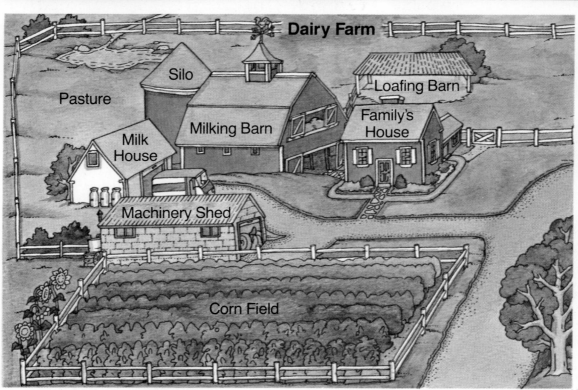

Dairy Farm

Pasture

Silo

Loafing Barn

Milk House

Milking Barn

Family's House

Machinery Shed

Corn Field

109

Dairy cows eat a lot of food. The farmers feed them good food. When a cow is well fed, it gives good milk. The milk tastes good.

Later, the milk is taken from the milk house. It is put into a big truck. The truck takes the milk to a creamery. A creamery does many different things with milk. You will read about this next.

● What kind of cattle gives milk?
● Are cows milked in the morning or evening?

Lesson 7: How Butter and Cheese Are Made from Milk

At the creamery, the milk is pasteurized. That means it is heated in a big machine. This is done to kill any germs in the milk.

Then, some milk goes to a bottling machine. This machine fills bottles or cartons with milk. The bottles or cartons are put in a cool place. Later, they are taken by truck to stores nearby.

Part of milk is thick. This is called cream. Some cream is put into a vat, or big tank. There, it is mixed over and over again. When cream is mixed enough, it becomes butter. The butter is sold in supermarkets.

Other milk is made into cheese. First, the cheese makers let the milk turn sour. Then they separate out the curd. This is the solid part of milk. The curd is salted and pressed into shape. The cheese is allowed to age. Then it is packaged and sent to your store.

So now you know where butter and cheese come from!

- Why is milk pasteurized?
- What is the thick part of milk called?

Lesson 8: How We Get Fruits

Almost everyone loves to eat fruit. You know that fruits like apples and oranges taste good. But they are also good for you. We eat many fruits just as they are. Many fruits also make other foods taste good. Jams and jellies are made from fruits. Many fruits are also baked into pies and cakes.

But where do fruits come from? Fruits, like other crops, are raised by farmers. Most grow on trees. Fruit trees are planted in rows in fields called orchards. Some fruits grow on bushes or vines. A vine has branches that climb or creep. Grapes grow on vines.

Most crops are grown from seeds. But fruit farmers plant their crops in other ways. They cut off part of a good fruit tree. Then, they usually join it to the roots of another tree. Sometimes, they plant the cut-off part in the ground. That way, only the best fruit is grown.

Fruit farmers use machines to "feed" their trees. Plant food is called fertilizer. Machines are also used to keep out weeds. Young fruit trees must be trained to grow right. Some branches are pruned, or cut off. Some fruits are taken off so others can grow bigger. This is called thinning. Farmers kill bugs by spraying the trees with chemicals. They try to protect their trees from cold weather.

Finally, the fruit is ripe. That means it is ready for eating. Fruit must be picked carefully. That is so because it is easily damaged. Fruit is usually picked by hand. Sometimes, machines are used. Some of the picked fruit is sent to packing houses. There, it is put into boxes.

FRUITS IMPORTANT IN THE UNITED STATES

FRUITS		LEADING STATES
Grapes		California
Oranges		Florida, California
Apples		Washington, New York, Michigan, Virginia, California, Pennsylvania
Peaches		California, South Carolina
Strawberries		California
Grapefruit		Florida, Texas
Plums and prunes		California
Cherries		Michigan, Washington, Oregon, California
Pears		California, Washington, Oregon
Lemons		California

Next, it goes to your supermarket. Some fruit goes to special factories. There it is canned, dried, or frozen.

● Where do most fruits grow?
● Do fruit farmers grow their crops from seeds?

Lesson 9: How We Get Vegetables

You know that peaches and grapefruit are fruits. You know that lettuce, beans, and potatoes are vegetables. Carrots, onions, and peas are vegetables, too.

Have you ever wondered how fruits and vegetables are different? Of course, they taste different. But there is something else. Fruit trees, bushes, and vines live for a long time. But vegetable plants are grown each year. They are usually grown from seeds.

Vegetables are raised on farms called truck farms. Some truck farms are near cities. They sell ripe vegetables to city people. Other truck farms are far away. Often, they are in places

PLANT PARTS WE EAT AS VEGETABLES

PARTS	VEGETABLES	
Flowers	Cauliflower	
Fruits	Tomatoes	
Seeds	Peas	
Leaves	Spinach	
Stems	Asparagus	
Bulbs	Onions	
Tubers (like stems)	Potatoes	
Roots	Carrots	

where winter is warmer. The farmers there
grow vegetables during winter. They send
vegetables all over the country by truck or
train. That is why we can have fresh vegetables
all year!

Growing vegetables is hard work. Vegetable
crops need much care. Farmers must watch out
for weeds and bugs. They must pick the ripe
vegetables carefully. Many farmers work
together to ship and sell their vegetables. They
do this through groups called cooperatives.

● Do vegetable plants live for a long time?
● Where are vegetables raised?

Lesson 10: How We Get Meat

Where does the meat in your hamburger come from? All meat comes from animals. These animals are raised on farms.

Hamburger is a kind of beef. Beef is meat that comes from cattle. In our country, beef cattle are important in the West. There, they are raised on large farms called ranches.

Most cattle are born in spring. They spend the summer with their mothers in pastures. These are large fields where cattle graze, or eat grass. In fall, the young cattle are taken from their mothers.

Farmers all over the country buy the young cattle. They put them in feed lots. There, the cattle are fed corn, hay, and other crops. The farmers raise these crops to feed their cattle. Finally, the cattle have grown big. They are brought to stockyards. There, they are sold to meat packers. The meat packers slaughter, or kill, the cattle. The meat is cut up and sent to your supermarket.

Many farmers also raise hogs. The meat of
the hog is called pork. Pork is eaten as ham,
bacon, sausage, and pork chops. Like cattle,
hogs are fed corn. Some hogs also graze.
Farmers sell the grown hogs to meat packers.

Many farmers raise chickens. Most chickens
are born in hatcheries. There they hatch, or
come out of the egg. Most of these chickens
grow up in cages. They eat food such as corn.
They are fed by machine. When the chickens
are older, they are sold for meat.

● Where does all meat come from?
● What is the meat from cattle called?

Lesson 11: Farming in Other Lands

You have seen how our country gets food from farms. This is also true all over the world. There are farms and farmers in almost every country. But farming is often very different in other countries.

Japan is a country in the Pacific Ocean. Japan is crowded with people. There is little land for farming. Most farms are small. Rice is grown on about half of the farm land.

Like wheat, rice is a grain. But, unlike wheat, rice has to grow in water. So it is grown in flooded fields called paddies. Dirt walls keep the water in the paddies. Once, Japanese farmers did most work by hand. Today, they use many farming machines.

Nigeria is a country in Africa. As in Japan, most farms in Nigeria are small. But farmers in Nigeria use few machines, unlike farmers in Japan. Chocolate comes from plants that grow in Nigeria. Nigerian farmers also grow peanuts. Maybe your peanut butter is made from Nigerian peanuts! Nigerians also grow palm trees and rubber trees.

Norway is a country in Europe. Mountains cover most of Norway. So not much land is good for farming. Most farms are small. Norwegian farmers raise many cattle. Most of their crops are fed to the cattle.

Many Norwegian farmers have other jobs. This is because their farms are small. They cannot raise enough food to make a good living. Some farmers work as loggers. Loggers are people who cut down trees for wood. Other farmers work as fishers.

India is a country in Asia. India has much good farmland. But Indian farmers farm in old ways. They do not use many farming machines. India also has many people. Indian farms grow just enough food for everyone. Indian farms are also very small.

Indian farmers raise many crops. Grains like rice and wheat are very important. Many vegetables, such as beans and peas, are grown. Peanuts, pepper, sugar cane, and tea grow in India. Bananas and cotton are also important.

● What crop is very important in Japan?
● Does Norway have much good farmland?

WATCH YOUR WORDS

Find the missing word. Pick a word from the list.

Fruits farms wheat
Vegetables plow

1. Most food comes from___.
2. Farmers___the land.
3. Farmers plant grains like___.
4. ___are grown in orchards.
5. ___are raised on truck farms.

Find the missing word. Pick a word from the list.

hatch pork barns
dairy ranches

1. Cattle are kept in buildings called___.
2. Milk comes from___cattle.
3. Beef cattle are raised on___.
4. The meat of the hog is called ___.
5. Chickens___from eggs.

CHECK YOUR FACTS

1. What is kept in a silo?
2. When is spring wheat harvested?
3. What is butter made from?
4. What is fertilizer?
5. Are farms in India large or small?

USE WHAT YOU KNOW

Look at the drawing. It shows how much corn is grown in five states. Each ear of corn stands for 100 million bushels. What state grows the most corn? How much corn does Nebraska grow?

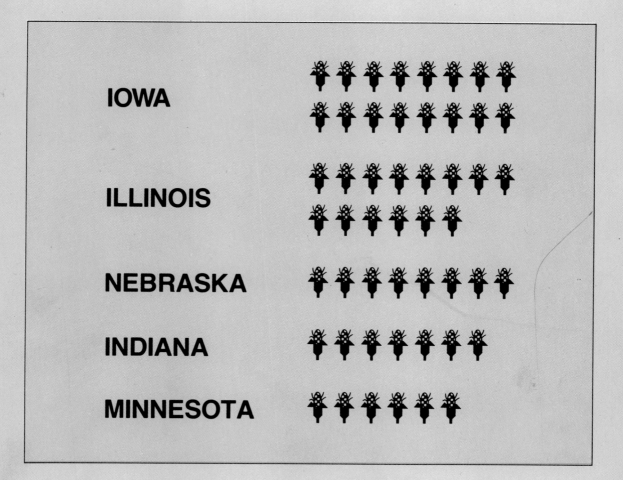

PEOPLE LIVE IN COMMUNITIES

Lesson 1: Communities Are
Places for People

All over the world, people live in
communities. Communities are places. They
have land, people, streets, and buildings.
Communities have places to live and to shop.
They have places to play and to pray.

Communities come in all sizes. Some
communities are small. They do not have many
people. They do not have many streets or
buildings. Such a community may be called
a village or town.

Some communities are big. They have many,
many people. They have many buildings. Such
a community is called a city. There are many
big cities all over the world.

People live in communities for many reasons. People need many things. They find many of these things in communities. They can get a house in a community. They can find food and clothing in stores. They can go to school or to a hospital. They have police officers and fire fighters to protect them. In many communities, people find jobs.

People like to live near one another. That is another reason people live in communities. They like to work and play together. They need other people to help in time of trouble.

● Name some things you find in communities.
● List some reasons people live in communities.

Lesson 2: People Start Communities

People started most communities in our country long ago. People ask many questions when they start communities. Will this be a good place to live? Can we make a living here? Can we get the things we need here? Can we sell the things we grow or make here? Suppose all these answers are "yes." Then, people have found a good place to live.

Many communities were started near the oceans. Some people could make a living there by fishing. Others could farm or cut down trees. Ships could sail to and from the community. A community where ships come and go is a port. The ships could bring people in and take them out. The ships could bring in things people need to live. They could carry away many goods to be sold. So the community could be in touch with many lands.

Other communities were started by rivers. Boats could go up and down the rivers. They could carry people from one community to another. They could also carry goods.

Later, roads were built. Sometimes, communities were built where two or more

roads crossed. Then, many people could come to buy things they needed. They could also bring things they had to sell.

Even later, railroads were built. Then, people built communities near the railroads.

People in most communities need to buy and sell things. This is called trade. People often start communities where trading is easy.

● Where were communities started?
● What is buying and selling called?

Lesson 3: Communities of Long Ago

Long ago, communities in our country were small. Most buildings were made of wood. Streets were not paved. To travel, people walked or went by horse or carriage.

Mostly, the communities of long ago are gone. They were torn down. Newer buildings were built in their place.

But people like to know about the past. Some old communities have been saved. We are going to visit Williamsburg. It is an old community in Virginia. Virginia is a state. It is in the southern part of our country.

Williamsburg was started in 1633. From 1699 to 1780, it was the capital of Virginia. The government leaders of Virginia met there. Williamsburg was a very important city then. It was as important as New York City or Boston. Many buildings were built in Williamsburg for the government leaders.

Today, Williamsburg is a small city. It did not grow like New York City or Boston. But it is very interesting. It looks much as it did 200 years ago. Visitors can see how people lived in Williamsburg long ago.

Most of the old buildings have been fixed up. The furniture in them is very old. Some of the old shops are open. Visitors can go to see a blacksmith working. A blacksmith makes things out of iron by hand. People can see how barrels or candles were made. They can see how people cooked food.

● Where is Williamsburg?
● Did Williamsburg grow much over the years?

Lesson 4: Communities Change

Some small communities grow into big cities. Others stay small. Some big communities grow even bigger. Others get smaller. Why do communities change?

Communities must help people fill their needs. Most people need jobs. On jobs, people earn money. They use this money to buy the things they need to live. Suppose a community has jobs. Then, people will go there to get the jobs. So the community will grow.

When new people move into a community, they need things. They need homes, stores, schools, hospitals, and streets. They need police officers and fire fighters to protect them. Taking care of these needs creates more jobs. So even more people come to the community. The community keeps on growing.

Sometimes, people leave a community. The community may get smaller. This happens when a community no longer meets everyone's needs.

Sometimes, communities lose jobs. Factories may get old. The owners may have to close the factories. The workers may lose their jobs.

People cannot stay too long in a community without jobs. So they move away. When people move away, stores, schools, and hospitals may close. Not so many police officers and fire fighters may be needed. Then, the community gets smaller.

● What happens when a community gains jobs?
● What happens when a community loses jobs?

Lesson 5: Big Cities Are Special

Big cities are a special kind of community. They take up a lot of land. They have large numbers of people. They have thousands of buildings and streets. They have thousands of different kinds of jobs. Big cities have many places where people can learn. They have many places to have fun. Some big cities have many different kinds of people.

Land in cities costs a lot of money. This changes the way buildings are built in cities. Buildings are built close to one another. They are built taller. They might have more than 1 or 2 stories. They might have 50 or even 100 stories. Thousands of people may live or work in one building. Buildings where many people live are apartment houses. Buildings where people work are office buildings.

Cities have many different kinds of businesses. There are factories. There are banks. There are stores and movies. There are companies that build buildings. There are companies that clean buildings or wash windows. There are even companies that deliver singing telegrams. All these companies have jobs. So big cities have many, many jobs.

In cities, there are many schools. There are elementary schools and high schools. There are colleges and universities. There are other places for learning and having fun. There are museums and libraries. There are parks and zoos. There are movies, theaters, and sports teams.

In cities in our country, there are many different people. Some are rich. Some are poor. Some are in between. Some people are Black. Some are White. Some people come from Asia. Some come from Mexico or South America. People in cities belong to many different religions. So you see many kinds of churches and temples. In cities, all these different kinds of people work together.

● Name some kinds of things big cities have.
● What are apartment houses?

Lesson 6: Big Cities in Our Country

Our country has many big cities. Look at the chart on the next page. It shows five big cities in our country. Find these cities on the map on page 145. Each city is special.

New York City is the biggest city in our country. It is famous for many things. Visitors love to see the Statue of Liberty. They love the view from the Empire State Building. They find Rockefeller Center exciting. They are interested in the United Nations Building.

New York City is known for making clothes. It has many big banks. It is important in television. It has many theaters and museums. New York City is an important port. Ships come there from all over the world. New York's nickname is "The Big Apple."

Chicago is our country's second-largest city. It is known for meat packing and for making iron and steel.

Chicago is in the middle of our country. So it is far from the oceans. But Chicago is located on Lake Michigan. And the lake is connected to the Atlantic Ocean. Thus, ships can come to Chicago. So Chicago is an important port. Chicago also has many railroads. Many

FIVE LARGE AMERICAN CITIES

CITY	NUMBER OF PEOPLE
New York City	7,000,000
Chicago	3,000,000
Los Angeles	3,000,000
Houston	1,600,000
Washington	600,000

airplanes fly to Chicago. O'Hare Airport is in Chicago. It is the world's busiest airport. Chicago's nickname is "The Windy City."

Los Angeles is our country's third-largest city. It is famous for making airplanes. Many movies and TV shows are made in Hollywood. Hollywood is a part of Los Angeles. It is called "The Entertainment Capital." Los Angeles is more spread out than New York.

Houston is sometimes called "The Energy Capital." Much of our country's energy comes from oil and gas. Many big oil and gas companies are in Houston. Much oil and gas is found near Houston. Houston is very spread out. It covers more land than Los Angeles.

Washington is a very special city. Washington is our nation's capital. The leaders of our government meet in Washington. The President lives in Washington. Washington is named after George Washington. He was the first President of our country. The city of Washington is not in any state. It is in a special area, the District of Columbia. So Washington is often called "DC."

● What is our country's largest city?
● What is special about Washington?

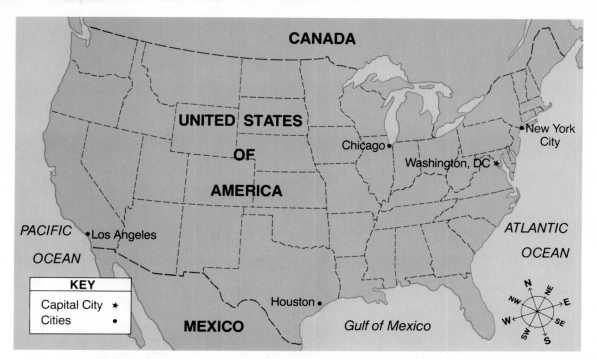

KEY
Capital City ★
Cities •

Lesson 7: Cities in Other Lands

There are big cities all over the world. Each one is special. We are going to visit a few of these cities. Find them on the map.

Tokyo is the capital of Japan. It is the biggest city in Japan. Indeed, it is the third-largest city in the world. Tokyo is a very crowded city. Look at the picture above.

Oslo is the capital of Norway. It is also the center of business in that country. Oslo is a

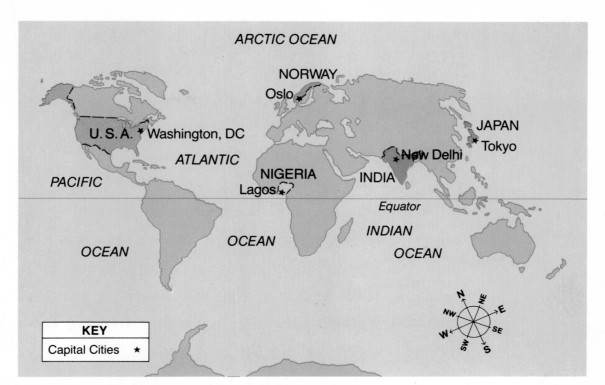

very beautiful, clean city. Look at the picture of Oslo on page 147.

Oslo is the largest city in Norway. But Oslo is not a big city compared to Tokyo. It is much smaller than Tokyo. All the people in Norway could fit into Tokyo. And they would fill only half the city!

Lagos is the capital and biggest city of Nigeria. It is on the Atlantic Ocean. Many ships come to Lagos. They carry away much oil. They bring in food and other goods. Lagos is growing very fast. Many people move there, looking for jobs. Look at the picture of Lagos below.

New Delhi is the capital of India. India has
many people and many large, old cities. But
New Delhi is not a very large city. It is also
new. New Delhi is a beautiful city. It has wide
streets and many large government buildings.
Look at the picture of New Delhi above.

- Is Oslo bigger or smaller than Tokyo?
- What city is the capital of India?

UNIT REVIEW

✓**WATCH YOUR WORDS**

Find the missing word. Pick a word from the list.

businesses trade apartment communities Cities

1. Most people live in___.
2. ___are big communities.
3. Buying and selling things is called___.
4. Cities have many different___.
5. Many people live in an___ house.

✓**CHECK YOUR FACTS**

1. Give two names for a small community.
2. What is a port?
3. Do communities ever get smaller?
4. What city is our country's capital?
5. Where is Tokyo? Where is Lagos?

USE WHAT YOU KNOW

Look at this map. It shows cities A, B, C, and D. Tell why you think people started each city.

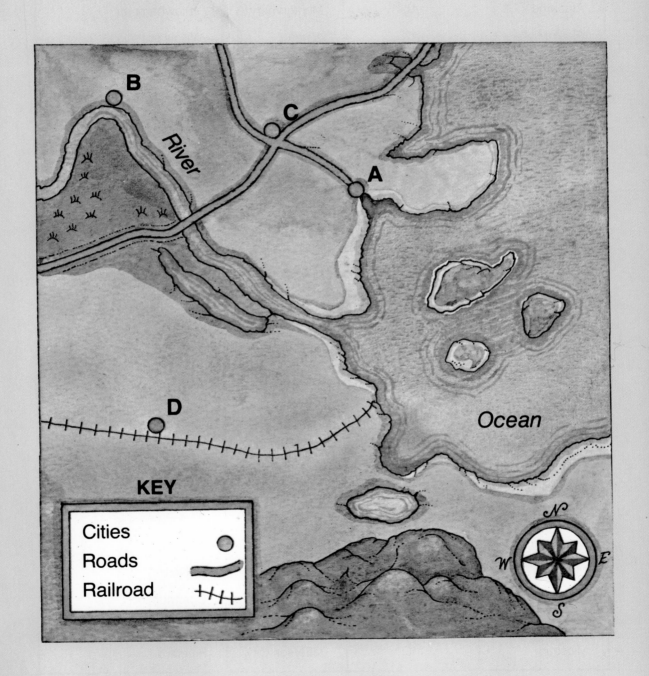

KEY

Cities ●
Roads ～
Railroad +++

River

Ocean

B

C

A

D

N
W E
S

FIFTY STATES CHART

State	Abbreviation	Capital City	State Bird
Alabama	AL	Montgomery	Yellowhammer
Alaska	AK	Juneau	Willow ptarmigan
Arizona	AZ	Phoenix	Cactus wren
Arkansas	AR	Little Rock	Mockingbird
California	CA	Sacramento	California valley quail
Colorado	CO	Denver	Lark bunting
Connecticut	CT	Hartford	Robin
Delaware	DE	Dover	Blue hen chicken
Florida	FL	Tallahassee	Mockingbird
Georgia	GA	Atlanta	Brown thrasher
Hawaii	HI	Honolulu	Nene, or Hawaiian goose
Idaho	ID	Boise	Mountain bluebird
Illinois	IL	Springfield	Cardinal
Indiana	IN	Indianapolis	Cardinal
Iowa	IA	Des Moines	Eastern goldfinch
Kansas	KS	Topeka	Western meadow lark
Kentucky	KY	Frankfort	Kentucky cardinal
Louisiana	LA	Baton Rouge	Brown pelican
Maine	ME	Augusta	Chickadee
Maryland	MD	Annapolis	Baltimore oriole
Massachusetts	MA	Boston	Chickadee
Michigan	MI	Lansing	Robin
Minnesota	MN	St. Paul	Common loon
Mississippi	MS	Jackson	Mockingbird
Missouri	MO	Jefferson City	Bluebird

State Flower	State Tree	Admitted to the Union
Camellia	Southern, or longleaf, pine	1819
Forget-me-not	Sitka spruce	1959
Saguaro (Giant cactus)	Paloverde	1912
Apple blossom	Pine	1836
Golden poppy	California redwood	1850
Rocky Mountain columbine	Blue spruce	1876
Mountain laurel	White oak	1788
Peach blossom	American holly	1787
Orange blossom	Cabbage, or Sabal, palm	1845
Cherokee rose	Live oak	1788
Hibiscus	Kukui	1959
Syringa (Mock orange)	Western white pine	1890
Native violet	White oak	1818
Peony	Tulip tree, or yellow poplar	1816
Wild rose	Oak	1846
Sunflower	Cottonwood	1861
Goldenrod	Kentucky coffeetree	1792
Magnolia	Bald cypress	1812
White pine cone and tassel	White pine	1820
Black-eyed Susan	White, or Wye, oak	1788
Arbutus	American Elm	1788
Apple blossom	White pine	1837
Pink and white lady's slipper	Norway, or red, pine	1858
Magnolia	Magnolia	1817
Hawthorn	Flowering dogwood	1821

FIFTY STATES CHART

State	Abbreviation	Capital City	State Bird
Montana	MT	Helena	Western meadow lark
Nebraska	NE	Lincoln	Western meadow lark
Nevada	NV	Carson City	Mountain Bluebird
New Hampshire	NH	Concord	Purple finch
New Jersey	NJ	Trenton	Eastern goldfinch
New Mexico	NM	Santa Fe	Roadrunner
New York	NY	Albany	Bluebird
North Carolina	NC	Raleigh	Cardinal
North Dakota	ND	Bismarck	Western meadow lark
Ohio	OH	Columbus	Cardinal
Oklahoma	OK	Oklahoma City	Scissor-tailed flycatcher
Oregon	OR	Salem	Western meadow lark
Pennsylvania	PA	Harrisburg	Ruffed grouse
Rhode Island	RI	Providence	Rhode Island Red
South Carolina	SC	Columbia	Carolina wren
South Dakota	SD	Pierre	Ring-necked pheasant
Tennessee	TN	Nashville	Mockingbird
Texas	TX	Austin	Mockingbird
Utah	UT	Salt Lake City	Sea gull
Vermont	VT	Montpelier	Hermit thrush
Virginia	VA	Richmond	Cardinal
Washington	WA	Olympia	Willow goldfinch
West Virginia	WV	Charleston	Cardinal
Wisconsin	WI	Madison	Robin
Wyoming	WY	Cheyenne	Meadow lark

State Flower	State Tree	Admitted to the Union
Bitterroot	Ponderosa pine	1889
Goldenrod	Cottonwood	1867
Sagebrush	Single-leaf piñon	1864
Purple lilac	White birch	1788
Purple violet	Red oak	1787
Yucca flower	Piñon, or nut pine	1912
Rose	Sugar maple	1788
Flowering dogwood	Pine	1789
Wild prairie rose	American elm	1889
Scarlet carnation	Buckeye	1803
Mistletoe	Redbud	1907
Oregon grape	Douglas fir	1859
Mountain laurel	Hemlock	1787
Violet	Red maple	1790
Carolina jessamine	Palmetto	1788
American pasqueflower	Black Hills spruce	1889
Iris	Tulip poplar	1796
Bluebonnet	Pecan	1845
Sego lily	Blue spruce	1896
Red clover	Sugar maple	1791
Dogwood	Dogwood	1788
Coast rhododendron	Western hemlock	1889
Rhododendron	Sugar maple	1863
Wood violet	Sugar maple	1848
Indian paintbrush	Cottonwood	1890

GLOSSARY

air conditioning a system that cools the air inside or indoors (98)

air pollution dirt in the air (86)

apartment a home that is in the same building with other homes (86)

apartment house a building where many people live (139)

bakery a place where people make bread (106)

barn the building on a farm where cattle and hay are kept (95)

beef meat that comes from cattle (120)

blacksmith a person who makes things out of iron by hand (136)

bottling machine a machine that fills bottles or cartons with milk (111)

builder a person who makes and sells buildings (74)

business 1 a person's job or type of work **2** a place where work is done (140)

butter what cream becomes when it is mixed and becomes thick (112)

capital the city where government leaders meet (134)

cattle cows and bulls (120)

central heating heating a whole building from only one spot (98)

city a very big community with many people and many buildings (21, 130)

cloth material that is made when threads are woven together (80)

coast a part of Earth that touches the ocean (33)

combine a big machine that cuts wheat. It separates the grain and pours it into a truck. (104)

community the place where a group of people live (130)

compass arrows that show directions on a map (18)

continent one of the seven large areas of land on Earth (24)

cooperative a group of farmers who work together to ship and sell their crops (119)

country a group of people with their own government and their own land (26)

cream the thick part of milk (112)

creamery the place where milk is taken for pasteurizing. Butter and cheese are also made there. (110)

crops plants that are grown on farms (97)

curd the solid part of milk that is taken from the milk when it turns sour. It is made into cheese. (112)

dairy cattle cows that give milk (108, 110)

dairy farm a farm where dairy cattle are raised (108)

desert land that is covered with lots of bare rocks and sand. It is very hot there and almost no rain falls. (36)

direction the way you point or move. North, south, east, west, left, right, up, and down are directions. (18)

disk harrow a tool used on a farm to break up the lumps of soil left after the soil is plowed (103)

dough bread that is not baked (106)

drill a tool used to plant seeds (103)

dyeing giving woven cloth a color (82)

equator an imaginary line around the middle of Earth (23)

factory a place where many people work to make things (73, 76)

family a group of people who are kin to each other (54)

farm a piece of land where food is grown or animals are raised (93)

farmer a person who owns or runs a farm (93)

feed lot a place where cattle are fed corn, hay, and other food (121)

fertilizer food for plants (114)

field a place where crops are grown (96)

flour grain that is ground up into powder and used to make bread (115)

follower a person in a group who is not the leader. A follower helps the group and obeys the rules. (56)

forest a place with many trees (36)

fruit a part of some plants that can be eaten. Some fruits are apples, oranges, peaches, and grapes. (113–114)

globe a round model of Earth (22)

government 1 a system of laws and rules 2 a group of people that makes laws and rules (134)

grain 1 a grass plant such as wheat, rice, corn, or oats 2 the seeds of such a plant (102, 123)

grain elevator a place where wheat is stored until it is used (104)

grasslands land where there is enough rain for lots of grass to grow but not enough for forests (37)

graze to eat grass, as animals do (12)

group a number of people together (51)

harvest the picking of crops when they have grown (97)

hatch to come out of an egg (122)

hatchery a place where chickens are born (122)

hay dried grass (95)

hill land that is higher than the land around it, but lower than a mountain (33)

hire to pay someone to work for you (76)

hoe a tool that is used in gardens or fields to get rid of weeds (110)

home a place where people live (74)

hospital a place where sick people are taken care of (73)

house a building where people live (74)

island land with water all around it (33)

job 1 a piece of work 2 the work a person does for a living (137)

lake a large body of water with land all around it (34)

landlord the person who owns a building (79)

law a rule made by a government (61)

leader the person who tells people in a group what to do (56)

loafing barn the building where cows are kept when the weather is cold (108)

logger someone who cuts down trees for wood (124)

loom a machine that makes thread into cloth by weaving the threads together (80)

map a drawing of a place on Earth (12)

map key a drawing that shows what the symbols on a map stand for (16)

market a place where things are bought and sold (96)

meat packer a person who kills cattle and cuts up the meat to sell to supermarkets (121)

milk house the building where milk is kept after it is taken from cows (108)

milking barn the building where milk is taken from cows (108)

milking machine a machine that takes milk from cows (108)

mill a place where grain is ground up into flour (105)

mixed farm a farm that grows several kinds of food (95)

model **1** a person or thing that can be copied **2** something made to look like or be like something else (22)

money payment for something (73)

mountains very high lands (33)

needs things that people must have to live (68)

neighborhood a smaller part of a city or a town (18)

North Pole the place that is farthest north on Earth (23)

obey to follow the rules and do what the leader tells you to do (56)

ocean one of the four large bodies of salt water on Earth (25)

office building a big building where many people work (139)

orchard a field where fruit trees are planted in rows (114)

packing house a place where fruit is put into boxes (114)

paddy a flooded field where rice is grown (123)

pasteurize to heat milk in order to kill any germs in the milk (111)

pasture a large field where cattle and sheep can graze (120)

pattern a drawing that shows all the parts of something, like a coat (82)

pen a small place with a fence around it, where animals are kept (95)

pioneers the first new people to settle in a place (98)

plains flat lands (32)

plans a drawing of a building that shows where the rooms are and how many rooms there are (75)

plow **1** to break up the soil, making it ready to plant crops **2** a big tool used to break up the soil (98, 100, 102)

polar lands land where the weather is cold all the time; land near the North Pole or South Pole (35)

pork meat that comes from a hog (122)

port a community near the water where ships come and go (132)

President the leader of the United States (58, 144)

prune to cut off some branches from a tree (114)

rain forest a hot, wet forest in tropical lands (36)

ranch a large farm where beef cattle are raised (120)

relative someone who is a member of a family (54)

rent money people pay to live in a home that someone else owns (79)

rice a grain that is grown in water (123)

ripe ready for eating, as a fruit (114)

river a long body of running water that carries water from the land (34)

role 1 the part a person plays 2 the job a person does (56)

rule something that tells people what to do (60)

season a part of the year when the weather is much the same (38)

seed the smallest part of a plant. When it is planted, it grows into a new plant. (114)

sewer a big pipe that takes waste water to a treatment plant (85)

shed the place on a farm where tools and machines are kept (95)

sheep animals with very thick hair that is used to make clothes (80)

silo a big, round building on a farm where corn is kept (95)

slaughter to kill (121)

South Pole the place that is farthest south on Earth (23)

specialty farm a large farm that grows mostly one kind of food (94)

spinning frame a big machine that spins wool into thread (80)

stockyard a place where cattle are sold to meat packers (121)

supermarket a big store where you can buy all kinds of food (92)

symbol a drawing that stands for something else (16)

tenant a person who pays rent (79)

temperate lands lands that are in between the poles and the equator. The weather changes. It is not always cold and not always hot. (36)

thinning taking some fruit off of branches so other fruit can grow bigger (114)

thread a very long, thin cord that is made when cotton or wool is spun (80)

town a middle-sized community (130)

tractor a big machine used on farms to pull a plow or a drill (103)

trade buying and selling things (133)

treatment plant a place that makes water clean and kills all the germs (94)

tropical lands land where the weather is hot all the time; land near the equator (35)

truck farm a farm where vegetables are raised (117)

valley the low land between mountains (33)

vat a big tank (112)

vegetable a plant or part of a plant that is used as food. Some vegetables are corn, cabbage, tomatoes, and beans. (117)

village a small community. It does not have many people. It does not have many streets or buildings. (130)

vine a plant that has branches that climb or creep (114)

vote to choose one thing or person when there is more than one to choose from (58)

waste pipe a pipe that carries waste water away from homes to a sewer (85)

water pollution water that has wastes in it; water that is dirty (85)

weave to lace threads together to make cloth (82)

weed a plant that doesn't belong in the garden or field where crops are growing (103)

wheat a grass plant with seeds, called grain, that people make into breads and cereals. (102)

wool thick hair that comes from sheep and is used to make clothes (80)

CREDITS

10–20, 29, 47, 65, 77, 89, 109, 115, 118, 151: Art by Jan Brett. **8–9:** Map by Continental Cartography. **21, 24–27, 43, 127, 143, 145, 147:** Maps and charts by Function Thru Form Inc. **22:** NASA. **23:** Robert Capece/McGraw-Hill. **30–31:** David Barnes/Photo Researchers. **32:** Cary Wolinski/Stock, Boston. **33:** (BL) Dan Budnik/Woodfin Camp; (BR) Monkmeyer Press Photo. **34:** (TL) Peter Arnold; (TR) Dan McCoy/Rainbow. **35:** C. C. Bonnington/ Woodfin Camp. **36:** (TL) Bill O'Connor/Peter Arnold, Inc.; (TR) Ronald Thomas/Taurus Photo. **37:** Bendick Associates/Monkmeyer. **38:** John H. Gerard/Photo Researchers. **39:** John H. Gerard/Photo Researchers. **40:** (TL) Hugh Rogers/Monkmeyer; (BL) R. Rowan/ Photo Researchers; (R) James A. Sugar/Woodfin Camp. **41:** (TL) Douglas Waugh/Peter Arnold, Inc.; (TR) Vivian M. Peevers/Peter Arnold, Inc. **42:** (TL) William R. Strode/Woodfin Camp; (TR) C. Vergara/Photo Researchers. **43:** Yoram Kahana/Peter Arnold, Inc. **44:** Marc and Evelyne Bernheim/Woodfin Camp. **45:** (TL) Tom Pix/Peter Arnold, Inc.; (TR) Jacques Jangoux/Peter Arnold, Inc. **48–49:** Mimi Forsyth/Monkmeyer. **50:** Richard Hutchings/Photo Researchers. **51:** Hank Morgan/Rainbow. **52:** Bendick Associates/Monkmeyer. **53:** Richard Choy/Peter Arnold, Inc. **54:** Freda Leinwand/Monkmeyer. **55:** Michal Heron/Woodfin Camp. **57:** (T) Michal Heron/Woodfin Camp; (B) Dan McCoy/Rainbow. **58:** Michal Heron/ Woodfin Camp. **59:** William Hubbell/Woodfin Camp. **60:** Jeffrey Jay Foxx/Woodfin Camp. **61:** Charles Anderson/Monkmeyer. **62:** Michal Heron/Woodfin Camp. **63:** Charles R. Belinky/Photo Researchers. **66–67:** Craig Aurness/Woodfin Camp. **68:** Margot Granitsas/ Photo Researchers. **69:** Bruce Roberts/Photo Researchers. **70:** (TL) Monkmeyer Press Photo; (TR) Craig Aurness/Woodfin Camp. **71:** Culver Pictures. **72:** Oregon Historical Society. **73:** Culver Pictures. **74:** Dan McCoy/Rainbow. **75:** Michal Heron/Woodfin Camp. **78:** Robert Capece/McGraw-Hill. **79:** Robert Capece/ McGraw-Hill. **81:** (T) Mathews/Peter Arnold; (BL) Robert Frerck/Woodfin Camp; (BR) Guy Gillette/Photo Researchers. **83:** (T) John G. Ross/Photo Researchers; (B) Jeffrey Jay Foxx/Woodfin Camp. **84:** Jeffrey Jay Foxx/ Woodfin Camp. **85:** (L) Hanson Carroll/Peter Arnold, Inc.; (R) Tom McHugh/Photo Researchers. **87:** Jacques Jangoux/Peter Arnold, Inc. **90–91:** Owen Franken/Stock, Boston. **92:** Grant Heilman. **93:** (TL) Jacques Jangoux/Peter Arnold, Inc.; (TR) W. H. Hodge/Peter Arnold, Inc. **94:** Grant Heilman. **95:** Grant Heilman. **96:** Grant Heilman. **97:** Grant Heilman. **98:** Culver Pictures. **99:** Culver Pictures. **100:** Library of Congress. **101:** Library of Congress. **102:** (T) Yvonne Freund/Photo Researchers; (B) Grant Heilman. **103:** Grant Heilman. **104:** (T) Earl Roberge/Photo Researchers; (B) Grant Heilman. **105:** (L) Erika Stone/ Peter Arnold, Inc.; (R) Dennis T. Gould/West Stock, Inc. **107:** Guy Marche/FPG. **109:** Michal Heron/Woodfin Camp. **110:** Grant Heilman. **111:** Sylvia Johnson/Woodfin Camp. **112:** (L) Earl Roberge/Photo Researchers; (R) Harry Rogers/Photo Researchers. **116:** (L) Cary Wolinski/Stock, Boston; (R) Jon Brenneis/FPG. **117:** Frank Siteman/Rainbow. **119:** (L) Joe Munroe/ Photo Researchers; (R) Owen Franken/Stock, Boston. **120:** Martin Weaver/ Woodfin Camp. **121:** Hank Morgan/Rainbow. **122:** (L) Bill Weems/Woodfin Camp; (R) Dan McCoy/Rainbow. **123:** W. H. Hodge/Peter Arnold, Inc.; (R) Yoram Lehmann/Peter Arnold, Inc. **124:** Anne Simon/Photo Researchers. **125:** Marc and Evelyne Bernheim/Woodfin Camp. **128–129:** Diane Lowe/Stock, Boston. **130:** (L) Freda Leinwand/Monkmeyer; (R) J. W. Cella/Photo Researchers. **131:** (L) Marvin E. Newman/Woodfin Camp; (R) Richard Hutchings/Photo Researchers. **133:** (L) Farrell Grehan/Photo Researchers; (R) Nathan Benn/ Woodfin Camp. **135:** (TL) M. E. Warren/Photo Researchers; (TR) Linda Bartlett/Photo Researchers; (B) Lillian H. Bolstad/Peter Arnold, Inc. **136:** (L) Southern Living/Photo Researchers; (R) Richard B. Peacock/Photo Researchers. **137:** L. L. T. Rhodes/Photo Researchers. **138:** HUD **139:** Jim Harrison/Stock, Boston. **141:** (T) Dick Durrance II/ Woodfin Camp; (BL) Wally McNamee/Woodfin Camp; (BR) Owen Franken/Stock, Boston. **143:** (M) Wasyl Szkodzinsky/Photo Researchers; (B) Jim Anderson/Woodfin Camp. **145:** (TL) Leonard Nadel/McGraw-Hill; (BL) Sam C. Pierson/Photo Researchers; (R) Carl Purcell/ Photo Researchers. **146:** Bob Davis/Woodfin Camp. **147:** (B) Dana Brown/FPG. **148:** Marc and Evelyne Bernheim/Woodfin Camp. **149:** S. Asad/Peter Arnold, Inc.